What a Hall of Famer Wants You to Know about Keith!

Tina Thompson is one of the most decorated players in women's basketball history and current head coach of UVA women's basketball. Tina's playing career includes retiring as the all-time leading scorer in WNBA history, a two-time Olympic gold medalist, a nine-time WNBA All Star and four-time champion with the Houston Comets. She was inducted into the Naismith Memorial Basketball Hall of Fame in 2018.

This is what Tina Thompson wants you to know about her friend Keith Veney

"If I had the opportunity to build a man in which I could put all the qualities that I admire: He would be rooted in faith, he would be God-fearing, family oriented, reliable, hardworking, honest, responsible, trustworthy, forward thinking, honorable, giving, caring, fun loving, forgiving, a bit stubborn, and living each day to its fullest extent. Good thing I don't have to do any building, that man is my dear friend Keith Veney. He lives his life in an admirable way, he leads by example and his successes are a testament to the things that he values." **– Tina Thompson**

Extreme Living

Extreme Living

Essentials Elements for a Transformed Life

Keith Veney, Sr.

SUDDEN CHANGE MEDIA
WASHINGTON, DC

Extreme Living: Essential Elements for a Transformed Life

Copyright © 2018 by Keith Veney, Sr.

ISBN-10: 0-9971609-8-5

ISBN-13: 978-0-9971609-8-7

All Scripture quotations, unless otherwise indicated, are taken from the *Holy Bible, New International Version*. NIV. Copyright © 1973, 1978, 1984 by International Bible Society. Used by permission of Zondervan. All rights reserved.

To purchase additional copies of this book online go to:

www.extremelivingbook.com

Please, email requests for more information or to book the author at:

keith.veney@bmhs.org

PRINTED IN THE UNITED STATES OF AMERICA

Dedication

First and Foremost, I want to thank God for being GOD!
Thank you, LORD, for all the pain, heartaches, failures,
lessons, tests, struggles and for saving my life. I have become a
better Christian, Man, Husband and Father because of it all so
I just want to say THANK YOU!!!!!!

Tyra Cook Veney, My wife of ten years! You are my mirror
and when things are not right horizontally you make me look
vertically for the answers. You truly make me better like Neyo
and Fabulous song and you have upgraded me like Beyonce did
Jay-Z while still being an independent woman like the Neyo
remix with Jaime Foxx and Fabulous and Yes, I know you have
your own............LOL! Thanks for sharing your life with me
and like we say, "We just getting started." Love you
POOHPIE!

Keith Marcel Veney, Jr. This book is for you! I wrote it because
you love to read like me so I put my thoughts and beliefs in
this book, so you have something to always read and reference
and it's something that can be passed down generationally. I
know you think I'm hard on you but KNOW Pop Pop was
hard on me, so I PROMISE YOU IT WILL ALL PAY OFF.
We have to always think BIG PICTURE and END GAME,
CHESS not Checkers, Stay Humble and Hungry.......Perfect
Practice makes Perfect.......and remember that HUMILITY is
matured in struggle and TESTED in abundance! JE PEUX ET
JE SERAI SUPER! JE T'AIME DAVANTAGE!!!!!!!!!

DELI DEL, Son you have no idea how you have touched my
life! Sometimes in life you think god has given you a burden
BUT in ESSENCE it's a blessing.......YOU ARE TRULY A

BLESSING and you have taught me to sacrifice, submit and be grateful for everything that I have. I'm excited to see what the LORD has in store for you. Be patient and stay the course because GOD is about to blow your mind. Love you Champ!

Ann Veney and Sam Veney, The LORD blessed me with the best parents for me! I know that I was hard headed and stubborn as a child. Mom you helped me lose weight for football weigh-in with those grapefruits and I know that's why I don't like grapefruits to this day, but you made sure I made that weight and Dad you told me DON'T GET MAD, GET BETTER and that's how I live my life to this day. So, what I gathered from those two experiences is by any means necessary GET IT DONE!!!!!!! I love you both more than life itself. THANK YOU for all the spankings.........LOL!

Reggie Veney and Conrad Austin, You two paved the way for your baby big brother! I stood on your shoulders and was able to see life at an advantage. Conrad, I still remember when I was eight years-old and I ran all the way from the park crying because you made me shoot the ball with back spin because I was using side spin so I started shooting the ball the right way the NEXT DAY! Reggie you told me to shoot the ball IF I PASS IT TO YOU and YOU BETTER MAKE IT!!!!!!!! LOL.....No Pressure for a ten year-old playing with fourteen year-olds........HAHAHAHAHA. So, to you both THANK YOU from the bottom of my heart. It would be NO McNamara Hall of Fame, Marshall Hall of Fame or NCAA Record for Three Pointers in a game (15) without you two. Love you Stags!!!!!!

Ralph Jackson and Alan Abney, My Brothers from another mother. We go back forty years to the sandbox and you both

KNOW EVERYTHING about me, so I just want to say I love you. BING, I'll see you soon for cigars and wine in your backyard and FAMO, Slurpee's on me Slim to celebrate so you both know whatever I GET, YOU BOTH GET!!!!!!!!

To My Village: Shimmy (My Right Hand), D.Simp (My Thinker), D.Clint (My Comedian), Moe (My Realist), Afiba (My Genius), Ren (My Jay-Z), Six (My Crazy), Denise (My RorD), OGary (My Business), LV (My Roomate), MMoss (My Fighter), Art (My Showmen), JPigg (My Youngin) I love you all for your differences and all you bring to my life.

To My Think Tank: Carlos, Abou, Tony, Alpha, Quentin, Alphonso, Dawn-Marie and Brother Curt Ashburn (My writer and publisher). Thank you for helping me write this book and flush out all the ideas from meetings with these, brother and my sister. I love you all and your knowledge, Understanding, Wisdom and BIG BRAINS!

Table of Contents

WISDOM

How to Transform Your Life with This Book

It is my hope that this book can provide you with an effective blueprint to transform your life. Let me be very clear, it is YOU, not the book, who will transform your life by the actions YOU take and the attitudes YOU develop!

All of the Essential Elements for a Transformed Life begin with the letter E and is in bold throughout the book. The E's are divided into three parts: Knowledge, Understanding, and Wisdom based on Proverbs 2:6:

> "For the LORD gives **Wisdom**; from his mouth come **Knowledge** and **Understanding**."

Each E takes time to incorporate into your life. For example, read **Exposure** on the first day and keep that E in your mind at all times. When you are ready, answer Keith's Extreme Living Challenge for **Exposure**. Now take a few days, weeks or even longer to practice your daily commitment to **Exposure**.

Move on to the next E (**Education**) only after you have started to act on Keith's Extreme Living Challenge. The next E must build on, not replace the E's you have already worked on. Keep in mind that transformation means your character as a person is taking on a new form and that takes TIME!

After you have spent months or even a year incorporating all of the E's into your life, go back to each E and evaluate how well you have incorporated that E into your life and "Grade your performance of this Essential Element."

You must be honest with yourself, remember, character is defined by what you do when no one is watching. This is YOUR life, you may grade yourself as you wish with A, B, C, D, F or 1-10 or even with words.

Then respond to the question, **"What game plan adjustments do you need to make?"**

The commitment you made the first time through the book was in response to Keith's Extreme Living Challenge, but now you should be ready to challenge yourself. Be **EXTREME**!

What does it mean to be **EXTREME**?

EXTREME

Keith's Definition

Going to great or exaggerated lengths beyond the commitment that 98 percent of other people are willing to make in order to live a transformed life.

> EXTREME
>
> *I love those who can smile in trouble, who can gather strength from distress, and grow brave by reflection. 'Tis the business of little minds to shrink, but they whose heart is firm, and whose conscience approves their conduct, will pursue their principles unto death.*
>
> **– Leonardo da Vinci**

Scripture

"I know your works, that you are neither cold nor hot. I could wish you were cold or hot. So then, because you are lukewarm, and neither cold nor hot, I will vomit you out of My mouth."

– Revelation 3:15-16

KNOWLEDGE

A wise man is strong, And a man of knowledge

increases power. – Proverbs 24:5

EXPOSURE

Keith's Definition

Exposure is everything we come into contact with in our Environment through our senses.

EXPOSURE

Avoiding danger is no safer in the long run than outright EXPOSURE. Life is either a daring adventure or nothing.

– Helen Keller

Scripture

"Do not be unequally yoked together with unbelievers. For what fellowship has righteousness with lawlessness? And what communion has light with darkness?" –2 Corinthians 6:14

Renew Your Mind

If you are exposed to a wide variety of experiences, it keeps you from being afraid of the unknown. Jewish children hear "Yes" 18,000 times by the age of 18 compared to hearing "No" only 2,000 times. Once you start to think life is YES rather than NO, you feel like you can achieve anything. Parents sometimes have an automatic NO response just out of trying to be protective, but really, by always hearing NO, children become fearful and tentative when faced with challenges later in life when there is no parent around. Childhood is a time when we can allow our children to experience things without a lot of real risk because we are right there to help if something goes wrong. Otherwise, our children go to school or hang out with their friends then go off to college having been so "protected" that they are either scared of everything or are not experienced at knowing a worthwhile risk from a dangerous one. Why? Because they lack **Exposure**.

Our children need **Exposure** to how to handle money, other languages, other cultures and to as many life situations as possible. Just as in a sport, the coach puts players in multiple pressure situations to expose them to as many possible game situations as possible. The same is true for life. Have a "practice plan" for your children so that they see the need for having a plan for nutrition, **Exercise**, **Education**, finances, etc. Be intentional about what you are expose yourself to, have a purpose. And parents, don't just be an ANT, an Automatic Negative Thinker. You shrink a child's world when you say NO, so when you have to say NO, make sure the child or athlete knows why the answer is NO.

Young athletes, you need to be intellectually curious. Parents, teachers, coaches, engage young people in dialogue so they are not afraid to respectfully challenge or ask questions when they don't understand why. Never answer a why question from a child with "Because I said so." A why question from anyone is an invitation to be taught. Don't pass up the opportunity. It's no wonder so many young people don't make eye contact. when they shake hands. Eye to eye contact creates confidence and comes from confidence.

Keith's Extreme Living Challenge

Why do you think Exposure is beneficial?

What are you doing in your life to gain more **Exposure**?

Grade your performance of this Essential Element.

What game plan adjustments do you need to make?

EDUCATION

Keith's Definition

To gain knowledge by learning the Essential Elements necessary for a Transformed Life.

EDUCATION
EDUCATION is the most powerful weapon which you can use to change the world. — Nelson Mandela

Scripture

"Present your bodies a living sacrifice, holy, acceptable to God, which is your reasonable service. And do not be conformed to this world but be transformed by the renewing of your mind."

— Rom. 12:1-2

Renew Your Mind

Education is essential to shape **Exposure**. Just having a lot of **Exposure** is not in itself enough. **Education** provides different options for every life situation that we might be exposed to in life. Your knowledge must surpass your situation. If you are looking to go to another level, you can't just stand still educationally. Potential is not the same as success. Success takes knocking at the right door, asking the right questions and seeking the right goals. **Education** prepares the ground for the seed that allows us to **Evolve**. To **Evolve** is to change so that we are prepared to act! Preparing the ground is hard work, you must do more than just absorb information. Teams practice plays over and over again against every possible defense the opponent might use. **Exposure** and **Education** are working together to create an evolution in the instinctive response of the player.

Exposure creates self-awareness and a hunger for more education. The same is true in the Christian life. **Exposure** to Christ and the Word creates hunger for more discipleship. The path that successful people take is **Exposure, Education, Evolution** and **Empowerment.** We have shown how **Exposure** is the ground in which the seed of **Education** needs to be planted. Now we will move on to **Evolving,** that is, how a seed dies in order to change from its potential to be a tree and grow, Evolve, into an actual tree that will ultimately bear fruit. So much goes into the life of a tree to get it to the place where fruit is ready to be picked from its branches. The ground must be prepared, the seed must be planted, the ground must be watered, the garden must be cultivated, and the tree or vine must be pruned. All that before any fruit is harvested.

Paul describes Christian discipleship the same way, "I planted, Apollos watered, but God gave the increase. So then neither he who plants is anything, nor he who waters, but God who gives the increase" (1 Corinthians 3:6-7). **Extreme** living is about the INCREASE!

Keith's Extreme Living Challenge

What is your next level of **Education?**

How will you continue to learn?

Grade your performance of this Essential Element.

What game plan adjustments do you need to make?

ENVIRONMENT

Keith's Definition

The conditions and influences that affect either negatively or positively the growth, health and progress toward a Transformed Life.

ENVIRONMENT

You are the master of your destiny. You can influence, direct and control your own ENVIRONMENT. You can make your life what you want it to be.

— Napoleon Hill

Scripture

"Do not be deceived: 'Evil company corrupts good habits.'"

— 1 Corinthians 15:33

Renew Your Mind

As we just learned, the path to success is **Exposure**, **Education**, **Evolution** and **Empowerment**, but between **Education** and **Evolution** we must talk about Environment. **Exposure** is the ground in which we plant the seed of **Education**. That ground is a garden that needs to be protected, it needs the right **Environment** to for the seeds to grow and **Evolve**. ALWAYS Protect your **Environment**. Society, what the Bible calls the World, is always manipulating our surroundings, always negatively affecting our **Environment**, always planting weeds in our garden. That is why we must always stand guard at the door of our heart and mind every day. Be careful about what you become comfortable with.

The most powerful influences on our **Environment** are other people. One thing is certain, when you hang out with another person, one of you will be changed. If you choose your friends wisely, you will both be changed for the best. Other people alter our inner outlook on life and that alters our outward life. Altering our outlook on life means changing our perspective, that is, changing how we see things. Remember, we don't see things as they are, we see things as WE are and who we are is affected by who we spend time with.

The question is whether the people we choose to be around are improving or damaging our environment. Protect your **Environment**, but when you can't choose your **Environment**, you have to change your **Environment** by altering your outlook. One way to alter our outlook is to ALTAR our outlook. In other words, place our old way of seeing things on the altar of the cross of Christ. That will change your perspective, things look different from the cross.

Our bodies are an **Environment** we carry with us all the time. We will look at taking care of our bodies when we get to the **Exercise** and **Eat** E's. But just as the body needs the right foods, but so does the soul, the self. We are not just bodies, but living souls, so we must pay attention to what we are feeding the Soul. The soul is fed through the senses, what we see, what we hear, what we taste, what we smell and what we touch.

Our soul receives information from our senses, so protecting our Environment means paying attention to what we feed the soul. As athletes, we know that junk food is bad for us and the same is true of the junk we take in through our **Eyes**, **Ears**, nose, mouth and touch. If we are around negative people all the time, then we are being fed negative thoughts and attitudes.

AA, Alcoholics Anonymous, calls negative thinking Stinkin' Thinkin'. Is what we are reading and looking at on the Internet nourishing our soul? When we watch violence on TV or the Internet we are taking that violence, simulated or not, into our hearts. What do we hear on the radio and hear and see on TV? Is it uplifting to our soul or does it drag us down?

What kind of seeds are being planted in your mind? Remember, scripture says that we "reap what we sow." You don't get oranges from apple trees. Do not think that you are an exception to this law.

Who is on your team? You are only as good as the people around you! Try to keep yourself surrounded by people that's doing better then you, smarter, humbler and hungrier then you. If you're the smartest person in your circle, then you need to change circles!

Keith's Extreme Living Challenge

List things in your current **Environment** that help you become your best self.

What are you going to do to enrich your **Environment** to an
Extreme level?

Grade your performance of this Essential Element.

What game plan adjustments do you need to make?

EVOLVE

Keith's Definition

To change or develop consistently and slowly into a better, more complex advanced state of being, a new reality, a Transformed Life.

EVOLVE
The whole point of being alive is to evolve into the complete person you were intended to be.
– Oprah Winfrey

Scripture

"But we all, with unveiled face, beholding as in a mirror the glory of the Lord, are being transformed into the same image from glory to glory, just as by the Spirit of the Lord."

— 2 Corinthians 3:18

Renew Your Mind

Once we have changed or controlled our **Environment**, we are ready to **Evolve** slowly and consistently. In a chaotic **Environment**, we do not have the consistency, stability, predictability necessary for growth. Do not delude yourself into thinking that you can step into greater situations while skipping over smaller ones. You cannot microwave the growth process. Evil is in a hurry, righteousness walks. Slow and steady wins this race.

There are lessons that must be learned and can only be learned through small beginnings with small steps. Yes, think big, but begin small. Growth and change are a process, there is a reason that we learn to walk when we are just knee high and not when we are fully grown. When a little child stumbles, the fall is not very far, so learn to walk before you try to run. Learn the fundamentals first, learn how to do the small things when the price of failure small. The CAUSE of our failure is within us, but the good news is that so is the REMEDY! Being unfaithful to the spiritual principle of small things first is the cause of much failure but being faithful to the small things is the remedy for overcoming failure.

Keith's Extreme Living Challenge

Why do you think **Evolving** is necessary?

List your next steps in **Evolving** as a person, athlete, son, daughter, friend?

Grade your performance of this Essential Element.

What game plan adjustments do you need to make?

ELIMINATE

Keith's Definition

To remove or put an end to something that is not wanted or needed for a Transformed Life.

> ### ELIMINATE
>
> *Art is the ELIMINATION of the unnecessary.*
>
> — Pablo Picasso

Scripture

"Then Jesus said to His disciples, "If anyone wishes to come after Me, he must deny himself, and take up his cross and follow Me."

— Matthew 16:24

Renew Your Mind

Eliminate ALL distractions that are obstacles to becoming your best self, even things that are not bad in themselves such as TV, radio, video games, etc. Use spiritual **Eyes** and **Ears** to **Evaluate** your activities to discern what to eliminate. It is not as easy as saying, "No more TV." It takes constant discernment not just blanket **Elimination**.

External things and activities can sometimes be easier to **Eliminate**, but it is often something like unforgiveness that needs to be Eliminated. Matt. 18:21 "Lord, how many times should I forgive my brother, seven times?" Who is the person that is stopping YOU from moving forward in **Extreme** Living? It's amazing how so many of us allow unforgiveness to ruin our lives. I know what they did is painful however we need to free ourselves from the bondage of unforgiveness now so that we can move forward. Who is it that YOU need to forgive? Do it today!

Eliminating negativity as well as unforgiveness in your thoughts and being disciplined about not dwelling on the past. People who knew you before you made changes in your life will not always accept that you have changed. They will hold you hostage to your negative past. Remember, the past will hang around as long as you keep listening to it. Nothing flees until it is resisted. "Resist the Devil and he will flee." Stop letting the past define your present reality.

Change is always unfamiliar, even good change can make us long for the way things used to be. Resist the temptation to be like the Hebrew people after God delivered them from the slavery of Egypt and said to Moses, "We would rather be slaves in Egypt than die out here in the wilderness."

Keith's Extreme Living Challenge

What things will you **Eliminate** from your life to become your best self?

How are you going to go about **Eliminating** the things that are holding you back?

Grade your performance of this Essential Element.

What game plan adjustments do you need to make?

EYES & EARS

Keith's Definition

The **Eyes** and **Ears** are the twin gates to our minds where the Transformed Life begins.

Scripture

"I will set nothing wicked before my eyes." — Psalm 101:3

Renew Your Mind

As we just learned, it is **Essential** to **Eliminate** the lies, the distractions and the unnecessary from our lives. We do that by evaluating with our **Eyes** & **Ears**. Every good and evil thing that the **Eyes** see, and the **Ears** hear transforms our minds so choose wisely what you look at and who you listen to.

Learning to listen and choosing wisely who we listen to is key. God's vision will stop us, send us and strengthen us. When David saw Goliath challenge the army of God, he was sent and given the strength to conquer the giant. But when David looked down from his palace and saw the beautiful Bathsheba bathing on the rooftop, he did not call on God to strengthen him, he sent for Bathsheba and committed adultery with her. He could conquer a giant, but not his lust. This led to the "man after God's own heart" committing murder in order to cover his sin. The eyes are the window to the heart. Be careful what you let in because the heart can be "deceitful above all things" and lead us into sin.

When Samson was obedient and kept his vow to the Lord, he was strengthened to conquer the Philistines in battle. But his vision faltered when he got drunk and let Delilah cut his hair which was his strength. So once again, a man of God could conquer the external forces in his life but could not conquer his own desires.

The appetites of the world and the flesh are powerful and addictive tools of the devil. He appeals to our love for what satisfies our selfish and sinful desires and uses it to tempt, control, discourage, defeat and destroy us. We also need to be aware of what others see and hear from us. Are we protecting the **Eyes** and **Ears** of those who are watching and listening to us.

Keith's Extreme Living Challenge

List what you spend time watching, listening to or playing on your devices. Grade each activity between 1-10 with 1 being not **Edifying** at all and 10 as Extremely **Edifying**.

What changes will you make to protect your **Eyes** and **Ears** knowing they are a gateway to thoughts and feelings?

Grade your performance of this Essential Element.

What game plan adjustments do you need to make?

EMULATE

Keith's Definition

To adopt and adapt the qualities of someone you admire, to imitate in order to become like another person or to develop a quality or qualities that they exhibit as a way to practice a Transformed Life.

EMULATE
Don't envy what people have, EMULATE what they did to have it.
– Tim Fargo

Scripture

"Imitate me, just as I also imitate Christ." – 1 Corinthians 11:1

Renew Your Mind

Eyes and **Ears** are on you just as your **Eyes** and **Ears** are on others. Can you say with Paul, "Imitate me, just as I also imitate Christ?" And we need to **Emulate** the people that are going where we want to go and make certain that you are the do the same for others.

When you do what is right you don't have to talk, people will talk for you. Adults tell kids to do what we say and not as we do. Shouldn't we be able to say DO AS I DO? What type of example are we setting?

Who we chose to **Emulate** influences who we become. Depending on who it is that we **Emulate**, we will either **Eliminate** negative attitudes and behaviors or have our negative attitudes and behaviors reinforced. This ties back into guarding our **Eyes** and **Ears**, being wise about who we are watching and listening to because we will **Emulate** them.

Then we have to ask ourselves if the **Eyes** and **Ears** that are watching and listening to us are being helped or hurt by what they hear and see. Are we worthy of being Emulated?

Keith's Extreme Living Challenge

Name three people that have qualities that you want to **Emulate** and list the qualities in each one that you admire.

Grade your performance of this Essential Element.

What game plan adjustments do you need to make?

EXERCISE & EATING

Keith's Definition

Being a good caretaker of the body that we have as a gift from God so that we might serve him.

> ### EXERCISE & EATING
>
> *I hated every minute of the training, but I said: 'Don't quit. Suffer now and live the rest of your life as a champion.'*
>
> — Muhammad Ali

Scripture

"Or do you not know that your body is the temple of the Holy Spirit who is in you, whom you have from God, and you are not your own? For you were bought at a price; therefore glorify God in your body and in your spirit, which are God's."

— 1 Corinthians 6:19-20

"But I discipline my body and bring it into subjection, lest, when I have preached to others, I myself should become disqualified."

— 1 Corinthians 9:27

Renew Your Mind

Exercise and **Eating** are necessary for a healthy life and having the **Energy** to be our best for God for however many years he gives us. If it is true that you are what you eat, then based on what you ate this week, what are you becoming? If you are not getting out of your body what YOU need, then you aren't putting into your body what IT needs.

To be great, be consistent in everything you do including nourishing and disciplining your body. Health is a kind of wealth in that illness or sluggishness steal from us. They steal time and money. Later we will explore **Energy** and **Efficiency**, two E's that are closely related to **Exercise** and **Eating**. Both our **Energy** and **Efficiency** suffer when the body is not healthy.

Keith's Extreme Living Challenge

Why do you think proper **Eating** and **Exercising** should be part of your lifestyle?

How are you going to change your **Eating** habits and **Exercise** routine?

Grade your performance of this Essential Element.

What game plan adjustments do you need to make?

UNDERSTANDING

And to man He said, 'Behold, the fear of the Lord, that is wisdom; And to depart from evil is understanding.' – Job 28:28

ELDERS

Keith's Definition

An older person whose life experience and wisdom are worthy of respect.

ELDERS
Children have never been very good at listening to their elders, but they have never failed to imitate them. **– James Baldwin**

Scripture

"He who walks with wise men will be wise,
But the companion of fools will be destroyed."

— Proverbs 13:20

Renew Your Mind

We need an **Elder** in every aspect of your lives. It might be different Elders that you turn to for wisdom in certain areas. I was taught to always seek wisdom from people who have gray hair. Gray hair is just a symbolic way of saying that a person has been around long enough to have faced a lot of different situations. In marriage, for example, find someone who has been married for twenty-five, thirty, or forty years. Scripture says that **Endurance** produces character and proven character produces hope and hope does not disappoint!

The same is true for your spiritual **Elder**, your financial **Elder**, an **Elder** for physical training. Some **Elders** will have wisdom in multiple areas but remember that "In a multitude of counselors is wisdom." Just on the physical training side LeBron James has a chef, a stretch coach, an agility coach, a masseuse, a shooting coach, all people he can trust. He knows each one has his best interest at heart.

Don't be discouraged if you think you found an **Elder** and then after a while realize that person has an agenda that is not right for you. Even if you get others to recommend an **Elder** to you, a good fit for your friend might not be a good fit for you. In your search, you don't want an **Elder** who comes across as one who has cruised through life without being bruised by life. That person is not being honest and won't do you any good because scripture says we learn from suffering and affliction.

Look for **Elders** who are humble enough to share their struggles because that shows honestly and **Endurance** and, as I said above, it shows proven character. The word proven here means TESTED. Their character has been put to the test and triumphed. Proven character produces hope and that's really what we are looking for in an **Elder: Endurance**, Character and Hope!

Keith's Extreme Living Challenge

Why are **Elders** essential to you becoming your best self?

Who are the **Elders** in your life that you look up too and why do you look up to each of these **Elders**?

Grade your performance of this Essential Element.

What game plan adjustments do you need to make?

EXPERIENCE

Keith's Definition

Experience is involvement through interaction.

EXPERIENCE
Character cannot be developed in ease and quiet. Only through experience of trial and suffering can the soul be strengthened, ambition inspired, and success achieved.
– Helen Keller

Scripture

"But be doers of the word, and not hearers only, deceiving yourselves." – James 1:22

We came across the admonition before to "Be not deceived." That was a warning that "bad company corrupts good morals."

Renew Your Mind

If you know and don't do, then you don't really know, to really know is to understand. Experience takes us beyond Knowledge (Part I) to Understanding. (Part II) That is, beyond Knowing to Doing. The most powerful **Experience** is first-hand or direct participation, second-hand experience such as direct observation followed by reading about something and the weakest experience is hearing or watching a video about something.

What's the deception if you are a hearer and not a doer. It's that we begin to think that if we hear about something, we can do it. No, you can't know that you can do it if you haven't done it. When great players are doing great things on the court or the field, it looks easy. That's because we don't Understand how much work went into developing that talent. We say, "Oh, I can do that!" Well, no, you probably can't if all you've done is watch someone else do it. **Experience** is everything.

When I set the NCAA record for most three-point shots made in a game, it felt easy, but there is a reason for that. I had worked hard in practice to know where my shots come from. I had taken tens of thousands of three-pointers since I was a boy. It only seemed easy, but there is a reason no one else has ever done it and why I only did it once. It was not a plan, it was a result of DOING the hard work over many years.

The more situations you **Experience**, the more defenses you practice against in sports or in life, the better prepared you will be to make the right decisions and do the right thing.

Keith's Extreme Living Challenge

List the five of your most life-changing **Experiences**.

What have you failed at lately? (By the way, if you have not failed at anything lately, you are not challenging yourself enough.) and what did you learn from your failure?

Grade your performance of this Essential Element.

What game plan adjustments do you need to make?

EXPECTATIONS

Keith's Definition

The belief (faith) that something will happen or should happen.

EXPECTATIONS
Put your expectations on God, not on people. – Joyce Meyer

Scripture

"Now faith is the substance of things hoped for (Expected), the evidence (**Expectation**) of things not seen." – Hebrews 11:1

Renew Your Mind

A realistic goal sets limits on what can be achieved. High **Expectations** set a minimum and with no limit to what can be achieved. We limit God just like we limit ourselves. We tell God how big our problem is rather than reminding ourselves how big our God is.

Our expectations for Christ are too low and that limits our **Expectations** for ourselves. "With God all things are possible."

Remember these principles:

- God is not thinking in small terms
- Our problem is not that our dreams are too big, but too small
- The person who does not settle, is the person who gets what they desire.
- He who compromises anything, will compromise everything.

- My plan B is to make plan A work
- We don't know what realistic is because realistic is based on opinion, never set realistic goals because whatever you think is realistic is limited by fear of **Expecting** more and failing
- Put **Expectations** on yourself not others.

Keith's Extreme Living Challenge

List three high **Expectations** you have of yourself. (Remember, if you haven't failed lately, your **Expectations** are not high enough to challenge you!)

Who in your life expects big things from you? Why and have you thanked them?

Grade your performance of this Essential Element.

What game plan adjustments do you need to make?

EGO

Keith's Definition

Ego is your sense of Self, of who you are, your "I" as in Identity.

EGO
If not to God, you will surrender to the opinions or expectations of others, to money, to resentment, to fear, or to your own pride, lusts, or ego. You were designed to worship God and if you fail to worship Him, you will create other things (idols) to give your life to.   — Rick Warren

Scripture

"Pride goes before destruction, And a haughty spirit before a fall."

— Proverbs 16:18

Renew Your Mind

An inflated sense of Self (**Ego**) deceives us about our need for change, a deflated Self (**Ego**) discourages us from believing we can be changed, but an honest and humble sense of Self is the first step on the journey to a transformed life.

Consider others...

- The people with the most pride, usually become the biggest swallowers
- To serve is to rule, to be a servant leader, serve so well that your opinion matters
- What do you have to give up to achieve your dream and reach your destiny?

- What is feeding your **Ego**?
- If you die to self, there is nothing God will not do for you, in you, through you
- Demotion to the world, promotion from God
- Do the things that other people won't do, go to places they won't go, then think like they think
- Satisfying your ego ultimately leaves you unfulfilled and less than your best self.

Everyone has an **Ego**. The ego is the MY in MYSELF or my Self. The **Ego** is that part of us that looks out for number One, it puts Self first and asks what's in it for ME or what's the best thing for ME, ME, ME, ME. Some people have said it stands for Edging-God-Out, **EGO**!

When a person asks the question, "Who am I?" the **Ego** shouts, I AM ME. Me, myself and I can handle anything that comes along. People whose **Ego** is out of control are called narcissists. Narcissism is named after a young man named Narcissus who had never seen his own face in a mirror. One day he bent down to drink water out of a very still glassy pool of water and fell in love with the reflection he saw not knowing it was himself, or his Self. The **Ego** is in love with itself and will always make selfish decisions unless it is controlled by something greater.

When Jesus was asked to name the greatest commandment, he said, "Love the Lord your God with all your heart, soul and mind," not "Love yourself." Then he said, "The second greatest commandment is like the first, love your neighbor as you love yourself." In other words, the same way your **Ego** puts itself first, we are to put others first.

We can only rise and conquer buy lifting up our thoughts. **Ego** thoughts pull us downward, selfish indulgence can bring temporary satisfaction, but the real winners, the great ones understand self-sacrifice, they lock up the **Ego**. When the **Ego** says, hey, take the day off, you earned it, you don't need to work out today, the winner tells his **Ego**, "Shut up, it's time to work out."

So, what controls the **Ego**? Well psychology calls it the Super **Ego**, but its street name is the Conscience. The **Ego** cannot be trained, it can only be leashed, chained, controlled. The conscience can be trained and in fact it is being trained every day for either good or evil. When the **Ego** says, "Hey, you are thirsty, have a soda," the conscience says, "Whoa, let's STOP and THINK about our goals. Let's drink a bottle of water." It's all about what we are willing to sacrifice, we can give up the soda or we can give up our dreams, we can't have both.

Keith's Extreme Living Challenge

What does it mean to have an **Ego** about what you do well?

What are you good at?

Do others think you have an Ego about things you are good at?

How do you stay humble and hungry at the same time?

Grade your performance of this Essential Element.

What game plan adjustments do you need to make?

ENERGY

Keith's Definition

Energy is THE POWER TO CHANGE either externally as in physical movement or internally as in a Transformed Life.

> ### ENERGY
>
> *Each time a man stands up for an ideal, or acts to improve the lot of others, or strikes out against injustice, he sends forth a tiny ripple of hope, and crossing each other from a million different centers of energy and daring those ripples build a current which can sweep down the mightiest walls of oppression and resistance.*
>
> **– Robert F. Kennedy**

Scripture

"Be strong and of good courage, do not fear nor be afraid of them; for the Lord your God, He is the One who goes with you. He will not leave you nor forsake you."

– Deuteronomy 31:6

Renew Your Mind

Physical **Energy** is kept up by proper **Eating**, sleeping and **Exercise**. Internal **Energy** comes from an **Extreme** passion and desire to be strong and courageous. Spiritual **Energy** is kept up by **Eating** the Word and keeping the Word.

Physical **Energy** starts with a good breakfast and spiritual **Energy** starts with reading the Word in morning. When you take that physical and spiritual **Energy** out into the world, people treat you differently. **Extreme Energy** is like a disease that is contagious. It spreads fast. High **Energy** people change an **Environment** from negative to positive. **Energy** is transferrable!

The other side is that low **Energy** people drain others of **Energy**. Don't be an **Energy** drainer and don't hang around low **Energy** people because they will drain your **Energy**.

God blesses those who **Energetically** seek him and everyone around that **Energy** is blessed. His Blessing does not depend on our success, our success depends upon his blessing. And his Blessing is for those who are diligent, those who with all their hearts and all their minds and all their strength, that is, our total **Energy**.

Energy is not just transferrable, it transforms. Look again at my definition of **Energy**. It is the "POWER TO CHANGE!" We know physical **Energy** comes from food. Where does spiritual **Energy** come from? Grace is the POWER, the **ENERGY** of God to do his will. That's why everyone is blessed by high those who bring spiritual **Energy**, it is overflowing GRACE for everyone who it touches.!

Keith's Extreme Living Challenge

Do people like to be around you and why and how do you know?

What type of **Energy** do you bring when you come around people?

Grade your performance of this Essential Element.

What game plan adjustments do you need to make?

EFFORT

Keith's Definition

A serious, sustained and diligent attempt to apply the Essential Elements of a Transformed Life.

> ### EFFORT
>
> *Excellence is never an accident. It is always the result of high intention, sincere effort, and intelligent execution; it represents the wise choice of many alternatives - choice, not chance, determines your destiny.*
>
> — Aristotle

Scripture

"Therefore, whether you eat or drink, or whatever you do, do all to the glory of God." — 1 Corinthians 10:31

Renew Your Mind

When the scriptures talk about strength, they are talking about **Effort**. It is important that our heart, mind and body are of one will, one combined **Effort** to achieve God's PURPOSE in our lives. Having a purpose is not the same thing as succeeding at that purpose. Success is for God to deliver. What he wants from us is the full cooperation of our will, total **Effort!**

Commitment and focus are required to reach your full potential (your true Self in Christ) and to carry out your purpose. We must commit to continual improvement through consistent and sustained **Effort.**

GREATNESS requires EVERYTHING we have, heart, soul, mind and strength, but AVERAGE takes just enough to get by.

We try to avoid the place of our best self because it requires us giving up our selfish desires, **Egos**, and our plans for great accomplishments

Whatever your purpose is, concentrate your whole mind on it. Put into it all the **Energy** of which you are capable of using. Rise by steady climbing and you will always reach the top of the mountain.

Keith's Extreme Living Challenge

Give three examples of how your **Effort** makes everyone around you want to give more **Effort**?

Can you leave everything you do with NO REGRETS?   How will you begin to make that **Effort**?

Grade your performance of this Essential Element.

What game plan adjustments do you need to make?

EXHAUST

Keith's Definition

To completely drain your physical and emotional resources, to give it all.

EXHAUST
When you have exhausted all possibilities, remember this – you haven't." — Thomas A. Edison

Scripture

"You have not yet resisted to bloodshed, striving against sin".

— Hebrews 12:4

Renew Your Mind

Don't take shortcuts, let up, back down or give up when there is still an ounce of **Energy** left in you. People fear failure and that makes them ease up before they have **Exhausted** their last option, their full **Effort**, Because, if they give it their all and fail, they have no **Excuses**!

People often quote Vince Lombardi as saying, "Winning isn't everything, it's the only thing." But that is not what he said. He said, "Winning isn't everything, but the necessary **Effort** IS." He also said, "The glory is not in never getting knocked down, but in getting up again." But he did say, "I firmly believe that any man's finest hour, the greatest fulfillment of all that he holds dear, is that moment when he has worked his heart out in a good cause and lies **Exhausted** on the field of battle – victorious."

Have no mercy, look within yourself and you will find slavish thoughts, slavish desires and slavish habits that keep you from doing all you can do to be victorious. Conquer these desires, cease to be a slave to yourself and no one will have the power to enslave you. Overcome yourself, if you wish to overcome adversity. Take the key and unlock the door that only you can open. Shut every other door except the one to your destiny, hallelujah! Go get it!

Keith's Extreme Living Challenge

How does **Exhaustion** feel to you after you have finished doing the thing that you love?

Are you willing and how would it change you to live with no plan B and only the determination to make Plan A work?

Grade your performance of this Essential Element.

What game plan adjustments do you need to make?

ENTHUSIASM

Keith's Definition

A strong feeling of excitement about something that you enjoy or desire that is reflected in your tone of voice, words, facial expressions and gestures.

ENTHUSIASM
The secret of genius is to carry the spirit of the child into old age, which means never losing your enthusiasm. – Aldous Huxley

Scripture

"And when the ark of the covenant of the Lord came into the camp, all Israel shouted so loudly that the earth shook."

– 1 Samuel 4:5

Renew Your Mind

Enthusiasm, like **Energy** can change a negative **Environment** into a positive one. **Enthusiasm** is also like **Energy** in that it is contagious. To stay **Enthusiastic**, we must stay challenged, keep bringing down the barriers and do things that keep our attention. People don't take you seriously until you are **Extreme**. If YOU want things to get better in your life, YOU have to get better. If you want things to change, YOU have to change. If YOU want things to improve, grow or increase— that's right—YOU have to improve, grow and increase. Those are unchangeable laws!

How **Enthusiastic** are you about **Extreme** living? How badly do you want it? Revelation 3:7-8 "And to the angel of the church in Philadelphia write, 'These things says He who is holy, He who is true, 'He who has the key of David, He who opens and no one shuts, and shuts and no one opens …. I know your works. See, I have set before you an open door, and no one can shut it; for you have a little strength, have kept My word, and have not denied My name.'"

Be someone who shows others the open doors and let's not shut the door of hope on others. And let's always look **Enthusiastically** for that open door in our own lives.

Keith's Extreme Living Challenge

What are you **Enthusiastic** about when you wake up each morning?

What could you do to show more **Enthusiasm**?

Grade your performance of this Essential Element.

What game plan adjustments do you need to make?

ENCOURAGEMENT

Keith's Definition

Saying or doing something for someone that gives them the courage to do what they need to do.

> ### ENCOURAGEMENT
>
> *Treat a man as he IS and he will remain as he is. Treat a man as he can and SHOULD BE and he will become what he can and should be.*
>
> — Stephen R. Covey

Scripture

"Be of good courage, And He shall strengthen your heart, All you who hope in the Lord." — Psalm 31:24

Renew Your Mind

Think about the literal meaning of **Encouragement**. It means to inject courage into another person. And then think about the fact that Dis-couragement means to remove courage. Wow! What a difference. **Encouragement** is a breath of fresh air, it gives hope, discouragement knocks the wind out of people.

There is a saying that people will often forget what you said, but they will never forget how you made them feel. Ask yourself if your conversations and actions add to or subtract from the confidence and attitude of the people around you? How do people feel after a conversation with you, **Encouraged** or discouraged?

Do your friends, siblings, spouse or children look to you for inspiration and **Encouraging** words? Light overcomes darkness. Do you bring light to dark situations or do you light up a room just by leaving?

If our horizontal relationships aren't right, our vertical relationship cannot be right. Scripture asks, "How can you say you love God when you hate your neighbor?"

The other side of being an **Encourager** is to be around people who **Encourage** rather than discourage you. Some people have so little hope for themselves that the only way to feel good is to bring down others. It is good to be around discouraged people and to **Encourage** them, but it is not good to be around discouragers, people whose mission seems to be to discourage others.

Keith's Extreme Living Challenge

List at least three ways that you **Encourage** your friends to be their best selves.

Name three people who **Encouraged** you in the past.

Who do you look to now for **Encouragement** when you are down?

Grade your performance of this Essential Element.

What game plan adjustments do you need to make?

EMPATHY

Keith's Definition

The feeling that you understand and share another person's experiences and emotions; the ability to show compassion.

EMPATHY
We must learn to regard people less in the light of what they do or omit to do, and more in the light of what they suffer.
– Dietrich Bonhoeffer

Scripture

"When the Lord saw her, He had compassion on her and said to her, 'Do not weep.'" – Luke 7:13

Renew Your Mind

The REM song says, "Everybody Hurts." Any word with "path" in it like sympathy, pathology, etc. has something to do with suffering. So, to have **Empathy** means to enter into someone's suffering. It isn't just suffering with, that is sympathy. **Empathy** is deeper, it is participation in the suffering and feeling it yourself. It isn't observing and feeling sorry for the person. It is what people mean when they see someone hurting and your heart hurts, too.

Our first instinct is often to give advice. To use words to comfort. But the first step in **Empathy** is to be with. Just be there. Hurting people need to know you realize how hurt they are at a level deeper than words. An old saying goes, "People don't care how much you know until they know how much

you care." Once that is established then **Empathy** can turn into
Encouragement.

Keith's Extreme Living Challenge

How do you feel when you see suffering in the world?

When things are not going well in other people's life how can
they count on you for help?

Grade your performance of this Essential Element.

What game plan adjustments do you need to make?

ENJOYMENT

Keith's Definition

To be filled with joy, a feeling of wonderment and satisfaction that goes beyond happiness.

ENJOYMENT
Far better it is to dare mighty things, to win glorious triumphs, even though checkered by failure, than to take rank with those poor spirits who neither enjoy much nor suffer much, because they live in the gray twilight that knows neither victory nor defeat.   — **Theodore Roosevelt**

Scripture

"The joy of the Lord is my strength" — Nehemiah 8:10

Renew Your Mind

The whole point of the last three E's is to bring a person to a place of **Enjoyment**. Our **Enthusiasm**, **Encouragement**, and **Empathy** should lead others to **Enjoyment**. **Enjoyment** is more than having fun, joy is a love of life that rises above both good and bad circumstances and always seeks out the next challenge.

The Teddy Roosevelt quote links great suffering with great joy. We have talked about suffering and self-denial in **Effort** and **Exhaustion** and all of that suffering is to lead to **Enjoyment** for ourselves and others. But it is also to bring Joy to the Lord. His Joy gives us strength and our joy IN him gives us strength.

69

Jesus said, "I have come to give you joy and joy in abundance!" Think about that. He said that the very purpose of God becoming man is to bring us abundant, overflowing joy!

We are created to bless God and enjoy him forever.

Keith's Extreme Living Challenge

What does **Enjoyment** look and feel like to you?

Do you **Enjoy** working hard?

If so, list three ways that you **Enjoy** working hard.

Grade your performance of this Essential Element.

What game plan adjustments do you need to make?

WISDOM

Do not forsake wisdom, and she will protect you; love her, and she will watch over you. The beginning of wisdom is this: Get wisdom. Though it cost all you have, get understanding. – Proverbs 4:6-7

EXCUSES

Keith's Definition

An **Excuse** is an attempt to remove blame for doing or not doing something to another person or for a reason not under your control.

EXCUSES

He that is good for making excuses is seldom good for anything else.

– Benjamin Franklin

Scripture

"If we confess our sins, He is faithful and just to forgive us our sins and to cleanse us from all unrighteousness." – 1 John 1:9

Renew Your Mind

Solutions not **Excuses**! Take full responsibility for your actions or non-actions

When life seems unfair, some people refer to a phrase that is not Christ-like: "Don't get mad, get even." My father's advice to me that I first remember him giving when I was twelve was this: "Don't get mad, get better."

Whenever I was going off about something that I thought was not fair, even as an adult married man, he would just let me talk on and on, make **Excuses**, complain until finally there was a pause and he would ask: "Are you done yet?"

That simple question reminded me that all my talking, **Excuse** making, and complaining had not solved one problem, hadn't done anything to make things better for me or anyone else. Then he would drop some Wisdom on me that would knock all the **Excuses** out of me. **Excuses** are a signal you give to everyone around you that you are defeated. That the problem is bigger than you or your God.

Here are a few principles to consider:

- The inferior man blames others, the superior man takes responsibility.
- **Excuses** are a sign of weakness
- If we look for **Excuses**, we will find them.
- Who decides what is too much to handle? The **Elder**, the coach, the mentor.
- Look for solutions, remember the words of Thomas Edison: "When you think you have done everything you can do, remember, you haven't."
- The solution is in the problem.
- Persist until you succeed. The Bible calls this perseverance.
- If you believe it is impossible, it is.
- If you work hard enough, long enough and smart enough, the impossible will become possible.
- Finally, and most importantly, the problem is not too big, your view of God is too small.

Keith's Extreme Living Challenge

What **Excuses** are you making that are stopping you from **Evolving**?

List two people who let you get away with making **Excuses**.

.

List two people who do not let you get away with making **Excuses**.

Who your biggest Enabler?

Grade your performance of this Essential Element.

What game plan adjustments do you need to make?

ENFORCE

Keith's Definition

One person (such as a coach) or organization in (law enforcement) imposing consequences for breaking a rule.

ENFORCE
The will of God will not take us where the grace of God cannot sustain us.
– Billy Graham

Scripture

"Now no chastening (discipline) seems to be joyful for the present, but painful; nevertheless, afterward it yields the peaceable fruit of righteousness to those who have been trained by it." – Hebrews 12:11

Renew Your Mind

Never underestimate the power of one person's Will to succeed. I was traveling with Scotty Pippen once and he told me that if a game was close, he knew the Bulls would win. I asked him how he could always be so sure. He said that Michael Jordan Enforced his will on all of us including Scotty. His will to win was so great that it affected the whole team.

Kobe Bryant once told another player, "The difference between you and me is that when I have to, I can will the ball into the hoop."

There is wisdom to be found for Christians in these two stories. First, if you are in the will of God, you can will, God will give you the desires of your heart. Second, strengthen your will by being around people with a strong will of good character. Lots of people have a strong will. That is not enough, it has to go along with good character. Few people have the luxury of being around a Michael Jordan or a Kobe Bryant, but there are **Elders**, coaches, pastors, financial mentors out there who know how to both **Enforce** their will on you and to strengthen you in your own will.

It's all about the mind. Our body will never go where our mind will not take it. Control the body and the mind will rebel, control the mind and the body will follow.

Keith's Extreme Living Challenge

Who are the **Enforcers** in your life?

Who holds you most accountable?

Who do you go to for wisdom?

Grade your performance of this Essential Element.

What game plan adjustments do you need to make?

EXPAND

Keith's Definition

To raise someone or something (idol) to a higher level: to praise highly.

> ### EXPAND
>
> *Here is the path to the higher life: down, lower down! Just as water always seeks and fills the lowest place, so the moment God finds men abased and empty, His glory and power flow in to exalt and to bless.*
>
> — Andrew Murray

Scripture

"Therefore, humble yourselves under the mighty hand of God, that He may exalt you in due time...." – 1 Peter 5:6

Renew Your Mind

Climbing the mountain of God is hard, it is all uphill. There is sacrifice and suffering, but the power to reach the top comes from surrendering to God for his grace is the power to do his will to the top of the hill. The closed doors and failures in your life are not due to bad luck but lack of training, lack of ambition, lack of drive or lack of desire. If there is such a thing as luck, it is the result of preparation and diligence. Your failures on the athletic field are not bad luck. Your marriage is not going downhill because of bad luck. Your financial woes are not due to bad luck.

If you intend to **Expand** and exult then never surrender to another person, always surrender to God. Before the American

Civil War, it was traditional for the general of a surrendering army to negotiate the terms of surrender with the general of the victorious army, but Gen. Ulysses S. (U.S.) Grant, demanded Unconditional Surrender when Gen. Robert E. Lee surrendered. There is no negotiating the terms of surrender with God. He demands unconditional surrender. He is 100 percent worthy because he did not hold back anything when he sent his Son to die so that we might live.

Keith's Extreme Living Challenge

Who is the person that can get you out of your comfort zone?

List three ways that he or she **Expands** you out of your comfort zone.

What is the one thing that you don't do that you know you should do?

Grade your performance of this Essential Element.

What game plan adjustments do you need to make?

ECONOMICS

Keith's Definition

The financial system by which goods and services are produced, sold and brought.

ECONOMICS
The time to repair the roof is when the sun is shining.   — John F. Kennedy

Scripture

"Owe no one anything except to love one another, for he who loves another has fulfilled the law." – Romans 13:8

"One who is gracious to a poor man lends to the LORD, And He will repay him for his good deed." –Proverbs 19:17

Renew Your Mind

Sixty-three percent of Americans are one paycheck away from financial disaster and cannot deal with a $500.00 emergency and most adults have less than $1,000 in savings.

The Biblical word for wealth management is stewardship. Notice I said wealth management, not money management. Responsible money management is part of wealth management, but wealth is more than money, it is the value of all of your possessions. As a general rule, it is important to remember that income is taxed, wealth is not. Just as in everything else there are good stewards and bad stewards.

The basics goals of being a good steward or wealth manager or steward are to:

- be honest
- pay your bills on time
- give to the poor
- be an owner not a renter
- be a lender, not a borrower
- have insurance on your car, health and life
- leave generational wealth to your children.

Some basic definitions are:

- Income is the money you earn
- Expenses are the things you spend money on
- Liabilities cost you money
- Assets pay you money

The Poor buy stuff, the middle class buys liabilities, the rich buy assets.

Remember the first E of Wisdom was **Excuses** and I said that your financial woes are not caused by bad luck? I can imagine you asking if it isn't bad luck to lose your job or that the stock market crashes or house prices go down. Those events might not be under your control, but it isn't bad luck if you are prepared for bad things to happen. Remember we said that if there is such a thing as good luck, it is the result of preparation and diligence? Well, that is true of **Economics**.

You have to plan for the day you are laid off. That means paying yourself first out of each pay check. You should not be investing in the stock market with money that you cannot afford to lose. The house you buy should have a mortgage that is no more than thirty percent of your monthly income.

Finally, buying assets rather than taking on liabilities will ensure that you have wealth to pass on to the next generation. In other words, PLAN, PLAN, PLAN. The old saying is true: Failing to plan is planning to fail.

If you do not know how to manage money or to accumulate wealth, go back to the concept of learning from an **Elder**. Find an **Elder** who is older and has been a successful life-long wealth manager.

Keith's Extreme Living Challenge

Do you have a Budget? Emergency fund? Assets? Does it include retirement?

The Bible says nothing about retirement so how will you serve others later in life?

Grade your performance of this Essential Element.

What game plan adjustments do you need to make?

EDIFY & EXHORT

Keith's Definition

To build up a group or individual, to increase the value or self-esteem of a person.

EDIFY
When we evaluate the rightness or wrongness of actions or behavior, we need to ask ourselves if that behavior will edify—build up—ourselves or someone else, or if it will tear down. The question is not what we can get away with, but what is healthy and edifying. **– Myles Munroe**

Scripture

"So encourage each other and build each other up, just as you are already doing." – 1 Thessalonians 5:11

"And let us consider how we may spur one another on toward love and good deeds." – Hebrews 10:24

"But, speaking the truth in love, may grow up in all things into Him who is the head—Christ from whom the whole body, joined and knit together by what every joint supplies, according to the effective working by which every part does its share, causes growth of the body for the edifying of itself in love."

– Ephesians 4:15-16

Renew Your Mind

We need people around us, including the **Elders** we **Emulate**, to both **Edify** and exhort us. We also are responsible to **Edify** and **Exhort** others. To **Edify** is to build up. To **Exhort** is to bring attention to a behavior or attitude in another person that needs to be corrected. **Exhorting** also **Edifies** but it sometimes has to **Encourage** some tearing down first before building up. Just always remember that when we **Exhort**, we are to "Speak the truth in love." **Exhortation** must be down with humility even if it is done very firmly.

It is always important to discern the best way to **Edify** and **Exhort** each individual. For example, you might **Exhort** a friend to lose some weight out of health concerns. If that friend is a man, you can usually just say, "Brother, you're getting a little fat. You might want to cut down some on the portions." However, coming right out and telling most women they look fat is probably not "Speaking the truth in love" like it is with a man.

That means finding a positive way to deliver a negative message. How do you do that? Well, if it is your wife, you know that "with me" time is important so ask her if she wants to start running together or walking together every day. That's just an example or conveying grace while **Edifying** the other person.

You have to be confident enough in yourself and at the same time humble enough to build up others around you. We all need help confronting out sins and shortcomings. You CANNOT conquer what you WILL not confront. Notice that the power to succeed comes from your willingness to face your fears. To put it in positive words, you CAN conquer what you WILL confront, and we need people around us who are willing to **Exhort** us to confront our sins.

One last **Exhortation**: When **Exhorting** others or responding to **Exhortation**, watch your tone, Proverbs 15:1 says, "A soft answer turns away wrath, but a harsh word stirs up anger."

Keith's Extreme Living Challenge

Who are you pouring into, teaching, mentoring and growing? Describe what that means to you, how and how often you do this.

List all those whose authority you come under? Parents, Pastor, Coach, Mentor, etc.

Grade your performance of this Essential Element.

What game plan adjustments do you need to make?

EFFICIENCY

Keith's Definition

To do something without wasting time or energy.

EFFICIENCY

Efficiency is doing the thing right. Effectiveness is doing the right thing.

— Peter F. Drucker

Scripture

"To everything there is a season, a time for every purpose under heaven."

— Ecclesiastes 3:1

Renew Your Mind

Efficiency conserves **Energy**. This is true both physically and spiritually. **Efficiency** is concentrated **Effort** which conserves **Energy** and increases **Endurance**.

Efficiency makes up for Deficiency. That is why sports and life are filled with stories of less talented people out performing more talented competitors. The right way is the most **Efficient** way and it is the most **Effective** way. So, when the more talented person is less **Efficient**, he or she is then also less **Effective**. That's why little guys have been beating big guys on the court and the field since sports began. What is truly beautiful is when the talented person is also operating at top **Efficiency** like a Michael Jordan or LaBron James.

We should always be looking to shed the extra burdens we carry that weigh us down with busyness, worry, anger, etc. All these make us less **Efficient**. We become more **Efficient** as we need to **Exhort** one another to go from good to better to best. Each step is makes us more **Efficient**, but it isn't easy or normal in maturity to start out at the best, so take small steps and go from good to better and then best will come after that.

You can't climb the mountain of God dragging your dead old self behind you. Paul wrote: "I press on, that I may lay hold of that for which Christ Jesus has also laid hold of me. Brethren, I do not count myself to have apprehended; but one thing I do, forgetting those things which are behind and reaching forward to those things which are ahead, I press toward the goal for the prize of the upward call of God in Christ Jesus" (Phil 3:12-14).

Keith's Extreme Living Challenge

Do you pay attention to details?

How do little make a big difference?

How often do you ask for help and who do you go to when you need to hear the absolute truth?

Grade your performance of this Essential Element.

What game plan adjustments do you need to make?

EXCELLENCE

Keith's Definition

Doing the right thing the right way all the time with **Efficiency** and **Effort**.

EXCELLENCE
We are what we repeatedly do. Excellence, then, is not an act, but a habit.
– **William Durant**

Scripture

"I have heard of you, that the Spirit of God is in you, and that light and understanding and excellent wisdom are found in you." – Daniel 5:14

Renew Your Mind

Excellence is not an accident, it's a habit. You don't start out being **Excellent**. It takes work. The rent on **Excellence** is due every day. You have to be consistently good before you are **Excellent**. Progress has to be made every day physically, spiritually, mentally. You can't be weak in any of those ways.

Trust the LORD to do the right thing all the time even if it's not what you want to do or hear. The world caters to the FLESH. The spirit is willing, but the flesh is weak. To be Excellent you can't take days off. You have to put something in the bank every day so it is there when you need reserve strength.

God believes we are capable of holiness. "Be holy as I am holy." in order to receive your true blessing you must ascend! Those who are committed to God's call to **Excellence**, will at times find themselves alone, secluded from all those who accept being average. Reaching for **Excellence** requires letting go of anything that does not contribute to our pursuit of perfection. One reason we remain unable to be **Excellent** in everything is that we are attached to so many things that really do not matter. Some of what we are attached to is bad for us, some simply is a distraction from **Excellence**. Remember the ego wants to drag us down and is always **Encouraging** us to become distracted by a hundred different things. Don't fall for it! Adam and Eve fell for it, don't you!

How to know the **Excellent** thing to do and the way to do them:

- Break things down into their essential elements
- Stay away from average or "realistic"
- Learn from people that are already great
- Become a great listener and remain teachable
- We follow giants and world changers
- Stay around people who can add wood to your fire
- Surround yourself with people who can help you get to the next level
- Be with people who know how to nurture you to Excellence
- As you grow, your associations will naturally change
- Accept wisdom from people whose lives demonstrate **Excellence**
- Do not take advice from anyone who isn't going anywhere or has not been where you are going
- Seek out people who build up, who **Edify**, not tear down

Keith's Extreme Living Challenge

What do you think it means to do everything as though you are performing for an audience of one?

List three things you do every day out of habit.

Are these all habits of **Excellence**? Which one(s) are not?

How will you change the ones that do not mimic **Excellence**?

Grade your performance of this Essential Element.

What game plan adjustments do you need to make?

EXCEPTIONAL

Keith's Definition

A case where a rule does not apply, unusually good, much better than average

> ### EXCEPTIONAL
>
> *Never give in. Never give in. Never, never, never, never—in nothing, great or small, large or petty—never give in, except to convictions of honour and good sense. Never yield to force. Never yield to the apparently overwhelming might of the enemy.*
>
> — **Winston S. Churchill**

Scripture

"Therefore, you shall be perfect, just as your Father in heaven is perfect."

— Matthew 5:48

Renew Your Mind

If **Excellence** is a habit, being **Exceptional** is an attitude. Being **Exceptional** is not being an **Exception** to the rules, it is choosing to be **Exceptional** instead of average. **Exceptional** people do all the time what average people do some of the time.

Strive for perfection model:

- If you chase perfection, you will catch **Excellence**
- Don't let your normal be your prison warden
- We need to be stretched in order to grow (the tension of a rubber band is only good when stretched)

- God wants you to do the impossible, the supernatural
- No risk, no faith
- You become your best self through both good and bad experiences
- Stop looking for the easy way out and do the work
- We must work every day like our lives depended on it because… it does!
- You must do the things that only you can do (special gifts, pure will)
- We must reach for new heights and challenge ourselves (no one wants to be challenged anymore or to have to compete)

"I don't feel like it, But I will" How many times has loved one asked you to do something that you didn't want to do? Did you do it or not?

Remember, "to obey is better than sacrifice…."

— 1 Samuel 15:22

Keith's Extreme Living Challenge

In your line of work could I walk in and KNOW it was you who did it? What are the signs of **Excellence** in your work?

Do you guarantee your work even if the guarantee is not written? In other words, is your word your bond?

Grade your performance of this Essential Element.

What game plan adjustments do you need to make?

EXTRAORDINARY

Keith's Definition

Above the ordinary, very unusual; different from what is normal.

EXTRAORDINARY
Affliction is often that thing which prepares an ordinary person for some sort of an extraordinary destiny. – C. S. Lewis

Scripture

"Can you search out the deep things of God? Can you find out the limits of the Almighty?" – Job 11:7

Renew Your Mind

- Push yourself to the limit so your talent can surface.
- See the invisible, believe the incredible, achieve the impossible
- If we are operation in our best self we can change history, culture, community, etc.
- You can do nothing wrong and still do nothing right.
- Perform for an audience of one (Col. 3:23).
- We steal from God and the world when we live mediocre lives when we don't become our best self we are starving someone else's dream.
- What is realistic? Nobody can tell you what it is for you.
- Push through your limits
- You don't know what you are made of until you are challenged

Your lifestyle is what reveals if you are **Extraordinary** or average, great or just good enough to get bye. Life is God's gift, style is what how you shape it for his glory or for yours. The world belongs to those who say, not just "I can," but "I will." Being **Extraordinary** has to do more with nerve than with ability. Mediocrity is not about being average in talent, but in attitude. When the thought of greatness or the size of the challenge makes your knees shake, then fall to your knees.

When you are weak, he is strong (**Empowerment**). You can't do anything you want to do, but you can do anything God calls you to do. Then, your confidence in the Lord and the passion in your heart relate directly to your maximum achievement. What is passion? Passion is what you are willing to suffer and die for. Max out, I dare you!

Keith's Extreme Living Challenge

List three activities in which you go the EXTRA mile.

List three activities that you just do enough to get by.

Grade your performance of this Essential Element.

What game plan adjustments do you need to make?

EMOTIONAL INTELLIGENCE

Keith's Definition

The ability to harness emotions and apply them to tasks like thinking, problem solving and delayed gratification)

Scripture

"When I was a child, I spoke as a child, I understood as a child, I thought as a child; but when I became a man, I put away childish things. For now we see in a mirror, dimly, but then face to face. Now I know in part, but then I shall know just as I also am known. "

– 1 Corinthians 13:11-12

Renew Your Mind

Emotional Maturity looks at the big picture, embraces delayed gratification, takes the long view and develops critical thinking skills.

Ignorance is the root of misfortune. Our creator didn't intend for us to fail or live in poverty, self-pity or mediocrity. He blessed us with imagination, reason, inspiration and the capacity for **Emotional Intelligence**. We are created in the image of God and to be like Christ is to become fully human.

YOU are going to have to change what you think, the way you think, your daily habits, what you read, what you watch, and your conversation because these things will eventually determine who you are and where you end up. Your mindset will help you accomplish amazing things, make tremendous sacrifices, endure hardships, resist temptations and ignore distractions.

When your MIND is right you won't be content with mediocrity and you won't be content with "good enough." The ONLY thing holding you back is YOUR OWN stinking thinking and YOUR OWN unwillingness to see yourself as GOD sees you.

Keith's Extreme Living Challenge

In what ways do you just settle for less because you don't trust the process or the people in authority?

In what areas of your life to you seek instant gratification instead of long-term greatness?

Grade your performance of this Essential Element.

What game plan adjustments do you need to make?

EMPOWERMENT

Keith's Definition

To transfer or enable another person to achieve or develop the capacity to achieve a desired outcome through teaching, **Encouraging**, inspiring, etc.

EMPOWERMENT
Whether you think you can, or you think you can't— you're right.   **– Henry Ford**

Scripture

"Now may the God of hope fill you with all joy and peace in believing, that you may abound in hope by the power of the Holy Spirit."

– Romans 15:13

Renew Your Mind

If you have been practicing all the E's up to this point, you should be feeling a lot of **Empowerment**. You should be seeing how you can leave a legacy of empowering others. We become our best selves in serving others.

Ownership is the key: If you don't like your life, change it by transforming your mind and your body will follow. God works through your mind to generate **Empowerment**.

The more time I spend in prayer the closer I get to THE LORD! So, make sure you put your time in prayer. Much Prayer, much Power; little prayer, little power; no prayer, no power! As Paul writes in 1 Timothy 4:14, "Do not neglect

YOUR Gift." We are here to glorify the LORD. We all have a GIFT from the LORD! Something that comes easy to us. Let's use that GIFT to **Empower** others and to become the best version of ourselves.

The prayer of Jabez, "And Jabez called on the God of Israel saying, 'Oh, that You would bless me indeed, and enlarge my territory, that Your hand would be with me, and that You would keep me from evil, that I may not cause pain!' So, God granted him what he requested" (1 Chronicles 4:10).

To increase **Empowerment** and build your ability to harness more power, you have to work through problems and make great choices (**Emotional Maturity**) in pressure situations, problems and pressure increase capacity when confronted honestly and aggressively.

Power is like a rock which remains silent and unmoved. If you acquire power, you must cultivate stability. You must be able to stand alone. You cannot have command and control over your **Environment** unless you have succeeded in commanding and controlling your Self. Knowledge leads to Understanding and Understanding to Wisdom

Keith's Extreme Living Challenge

How will you use the E's to transform and **Empower** your life?

How is ownership of your life going to look going forward?

Grade your performance of this Essential Element.

What game plan adjustments do you need to make?